This journal b